SUSPENDED ON A LINE

Walter Battistessa

suspended
on a line

Foreword by Furio Colombo

RIZZOLI
NEW YORK

First published in the United States of America in 1992 by
RIZZOLI INTERNATIONAL PUBLICATIONS, INC.
300 Park Avenue South, New York, NY 10010

Library of Congress Cataloging-in-Publication Data

Battistessa, Walter.
    [Appesi a un filo. English]
    Suspended on a line / Walter Battistessa ; foreword by Furio
Colombo
        p.   cm.
    Translation of: Appesi a un filo.
    ISBN 0-8478-1481-5
    1. Photography, Artistic. 2. Clotheslines—Pictorial works.
I. Title.
TR654.B32613   1992
779'.092   dc20   91-33202
                                                    CIP

Designed by Italo Lupi
English language translation from the Italian by Hanna Hannah
The photographs were taken with Kodak Ektachrome film

Printed and bound in Italy

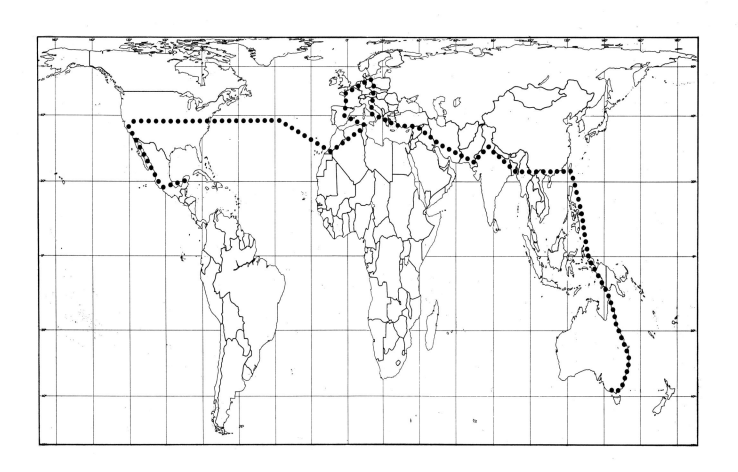

Furio Colombo

Interpretations of "Suspended on a Line"

There are many ways to identify the human presence. Scientific genetic formulas. Organic traces. Signs of the environment's inhabitability, such as data on other planets tirelessly reviewed by astronomers for their possible ability to support life.

It is from the cave drawings of animals, a first sign, that we begin to count the first thousand years. The calcified bodies recovered from the lava at Pompeii, proofs of life and death.

In these images the trajectory varies, and this is what persuaded me to write about them. The sign of life is pursued in a way that is simple, primitive and infallible: the washed rag, the clean, threadbare or faded rag. Rags, cloth, sheets, gauze, hammock, as signs of life and survival. And much more: a message of occupied space, of ongoing life, of health, of a person's affirmation over the landscape, of the difficult and rough conditions of existence. The fluttering of a bit of joy, of intention to remain, of hope.

More proof? When the Kurds began their terrifying march into the mountains of Iraq to escape the atrocities perpetrated by their own government, they left behind a trail of their blood, their dead children, their exhausted elders. They would never have been able to leave behind, as testimonial to their despair, a single one of these images. The sign of their march was death, not life, terror, not hope, anguished defence, not the routines of everyday life that create fatigue but also moments of serenity.

Here intuition is so simple as to appear banal: the rags themselves, left by someone for whatever reason, are always a proof of life. This is a reason in itself. First I must tell the reader the following: I am writing about this book of pictures because I noticed, looking at them carefully, that it involves an inquiry, an extensive investigation around the world, as in a thriller.

I didn't notice this right away. At first glance I thought the colors were very beautiful, the cleverly cropped sharp images always suggestive of something about to be revealed while hiding something else. The secret is to stay with each one of these photographs for a minute. During this minute the image changes as if there were some imperceptible movement, as if something had happened within the small lapse of time in which the shot was taken. I thought: this is a very clever photographer, it is worth following him in his game of continually shifting images, place, and narrative. And the narrative itself is what hooked me. I know this is typical of good photographs. But to state it is a way of highlighting the satisfaction one gets in looking at an intensely beautiful picture. The sense of narrative comes out of this persuasion: that something lies beneath it. It is something other than what I am looking at, otherwise the emotional reaction would not be as intense.

Much of this effect is due—admittedly—to the author's extreme calm and concern (but this is only a first impression) with not altering anything, not wishing to encumber. He identifies the place and situation, then retreats. One has the perfect impression of being the only one looking on. And if by chance a human figure is discovered in the picture, one is positive to have discovered it oneself, while looking, as if it had not been there from the first. And even if the figure is looking at you, if it makes you see something, if it sends you a signal, that instant of discourse seems to unfold between you and the image, giving you the impression of having arrived after the photograph was taken.

Walter Battistessa pulls this off with skill and intelligence indeed: he leaves you alone, he gives you the responsibility of conducting your own dialogue with what you are looking at. He sets in motion a magical situation in which it is up to you, facing each photo, to make discoveries.

One congratulates oneself for experiencing this, but one is still only barely at the margins of the full story.

I continue to glance through the book and believe to have found another clue: there are groups of photographs, groups of arguments, episodes delegated to a place, or a culture, or a relation between a person or persons, and the rags themselves.

For example, there is Naples or Barcelona, Hong Kong and New Mexico, India, Germany, Holland, Burano, Philadelphia, and Australia. Sometimes the concrete is emphasized, sometimes the water, sometimes the sky, or the rag with its more or less characteristic lightness and gayety, and its color that more or less transforms all the other colors.

The human protagonist, of whom the rags are a testimonial, can be the child that is bathing, the elderly person who sits waiting, the woman who is working, the man who watches. Perhaps it's some action that makes you notice a thing or the people who appear in the picture, or else the person turning directly toward the viewer with an action that he carries out for his benefit, or yours, such as the Australian who is flexing his muscles. Indeed, one can't help but notice that across the pages, across the images, a nexus links Venice to Venice and Hong Kong to Hong Kong, and some signs take you to Asia and others to the Casbah, yet others to New Mexico.

I quickly took note of the themes: the rags that are a testimonial to work, all those that say "toil," all those that signal "expectation," all those that speak of rest, those with a sacred or ritualistic sign, those that signal organized labor—the colored cloths that go from the weaving factory to be dyed—those which are a pure and simple indication of someone living there, that his life is not the rags, but the rags state that there, nearby, a life has been established.

Nevertheless, I suspect, these are not the themes that have guided Walter Battistessa's strange travels around the world with his camera.

The colors as well as the composition are splendid. But don't let yourself be fooled. The fact that the photographer is so clever at capturing the instant and the point at which the colors explode or come together in that particular image, the fact that his revelatory talent isolates that blue, that white, that purest red, that black, so skillfully, is testimonial to a verifiable reality that is there to be seen.

However, it occurs to me that there are false clues involved here. Not that this author wants to trick us. On the contrary, there is a "clue" within each image, one that points to another trail, another trajectory, another link. We need to come closer, go further in. And farther away. We need to discover where each part of the encoded message in each photograph, each color, and each rag will take us.

Only then, perhaps, can we come to discover what exactly the meaning of the element is that links this whole story and that is poetically expressed in the title "Suspended on a Line."

Which line is it? The rationale of a visual artist is never verbal. Let's follow him, nevertheless, along the very path, within his narrative of figures and color.

A first frame of reference—or trajectory, trail of clues for discovering the meaning of these images—is "poverty." I deliberately use this word instead of penury, indigence, misery, because Walter Battistessa's vision of the world does not seek excess but disdains it. He seeks normality. The life of the poor which here means the "non-rich," is close to nature and lived simply, which is the condition in many parts of the world. Because the photographer's eye follows the rags and their color, poverty is only one way of life among many. Whereas wealth is omitted from this trajectory, because, at least according to the author's code, it excludes the natural activities of life. Here nobody is rich and nobody is desperate. He presents his rags as a guarantee for next day's sun, as a continuation of life, more than as a declaration of necessity.

A path that crosses regions of poverty goes from certain courtyards in Naples to certain quarters of Hong Kong, to certain corners of the Third World, to certain hideouts of immigrants in Europe. In these images there is a lot of color, but it isn't "color" in the sense that this word is used to mean a deliberate "coloring" of life. I wouldn't say that the author is impartial toward life. It is his hand, his eyes that isolate and choose that spot, that play of shadows and light, that narrow slit that brings to view only the particularities of that universe.

But his intent is not color. He looks for color where it happens to be; one has the feeling that he has found and not invented it. He wanted to show it, not heighten or force it.

Let's see, then, what these colors, images, and snapshots that take us along the path of poverty have to say in different and distant places. They tell us that the regions of the world are arranged in a manner more authentic than the one we see on the map or even the one we know from our experience and our culture. Indeed, distant, mysterious, and exotic things do exist. But for us, the viewers, the courtyards of Naples are no closer than Hong Kong or certain scenes in India. We think of them rather as separate zones. Instead, it is from us that they are separate, but not in the manner in which the atlas points them out. The culture of travel is one of cultural identity that in these images deceives us; they are revelations to collect and save. "Near" and "far" are facets of an illusory perception.

In another sense the photographer's eye has seen nothing but a relationship between people and nature. This makes way for the presence of water, earth, and the sky. The wind and natural phenomena burst forth blowing up and changing the shape of things, and someone who lives in contact with nature is in a good position to understand them as natural facts. They give us the impression of an extraordinary governing force, the blown out rags, full and taut with the wind that beats against them, the light that penetrates and overwhelms color, the violent contrast between light and shadow in which the rags themselves are a link, the only unifying element.

I wish to clarify. When I say "relation between people and nature" I am not speaking only of those photographs in which the basic elements of nature and the forces that animate and disturb them appear. I am also referring to urban scenes in which a shaft of light changes everything, in which everything seems to have been waiting for that moment and that shaft of light, not only to make that photograph, but also to find the only possible point of equilibrium. Certain views of Naples, of the Casbah, certain slivers of light that shine through between black walls, like in a canyon, appear here as "nature." They are empty landscapes. They seem empty but they never truly are in this book because—we understand as we look—the author is convinced that they are "nature" for those who live in those places, for anyone coming upon that sliver of light.

But the wandering continues along still diverse paths. One of them, indeed, is the most extreme boundary, the frontier that links a diversity of views. In almost all the images of Australia, for example, the feeling of "distance" is represented in an agonizing manner, the images with baby diapers that flutter truly like flags at the borderline. Also some faces of the elderly, such as the old Indian woman in front of her American "pueblo" built with the ancient technology of the village, painted in that splendid way, the light of nature set in relation to the light of her eyes.

To live on the water, as in the harbor of Hong Kong, should mean "poverty," and it is in fact poverty according to those who have seen the sampans and those who inhabit them. Here, however, are other kinds of frontier images. The water, like the sand, is like all other temporary and uncertain settlements that seem to explain to those who live in palaces what life really is: one magical glance allows one to see it free of all social interpretations, an elusive anchorage, a liquid or sandy base, a continuous and uncertain fluctuation between rest and movement, between survival, with the few joyous testimonials of life itself, and the precariousness of being without roots.

But New Mexico and certain streets in Naples, the iron grills of the Casbah and the hammocks of Cancun that dry in the sun, are all outer frontiers in a little noticed world that is ours, an outer frontier from which we could have—if we knew how to see it—a clearer image of our existence.

Labor is also portrayed in these images. It is never indoors, it is never the process that produces a product. It takes place on the sunny terraces of Fez where cloth is dyed, or where it is already drying in the sun, or in those moments in Indian life in which something—between two moments of extreme exertion—appears to be splendid, appears as an explosion of joy only because of the colors, the rapture of the orange-colored gauze. There are Italian vintners or Mexican peasants, the signs of frenetic activity in San Francisco, the gazes that penetrate through the Casbah, trying not to get entangled in the extremely beautiful and abstract form of color.

Work is seen in these images in relation to the basic facts of nature, to light, and the impression is that this is the ultimate judgment and the only market that counts. The market of light.

But the only products possible here are the materials, cloths, veils, linens, things that can be made by machine or by hand, but that are destined to touch and be touched with the hands and body, to mediate between the human body and nature, and that are at least in part beautiful, delicate, consumable, rootless, similar to the life of the human being who produces them and extends them to the sun.

At this point in my trajectory I find myself facing an unavoidable thought. In Walter Battistessa's images, in his eye, in his point of view, even in his instinct, there is poetry. I mean a way of putting oneself in contact with what one sees and represents, finding a point of harmony that isn't obvious and that others do not see.

A typical outcome, when the poetic dimension of things is sought and expressed, the fatal and nevertheless quite frequent outcome, is a sense of emotion and deep feeling that almost immediately is identified with an intuitive conviction, a sense of sorrow.

For this reason poetry, almost always, in a painting, in a landscape, in an image, but also in a story or film, is also an anticipation of the end and therefore of pain.

Pain is not absent in this book, therefore one sees many eyes, many faces, many wrinkles, many patient and expectant glances.

But this is not the goal here. On the contrary, here the poetic glance is based on the author's mysterious but extremely obvious sense of harmony in the things he sees. He brings about a certain light effervescence, a sense of life, of celebration, of song. The rags in the wind are a sign of existence and continuity of life, they are the reassuring proof that someone is close by, with their work, their shelter, their children, their resting place near these rags that shiver, that beat about, that warm up, that are blown by the wind, that are resplendent in the sun or create shade, or that filter the light, or that alter the landscape or are blended into it. While one looks at these images over and over one soon becomes aware that they exude a light but full sense of euphoria.

If no other proof of life on earth exists to place in the steel capsule buried in concrete for the benefit of future civilizations or in the event of an invasion from other planets, Walter Battistessa's images would suffice—tenderly human and beautiful, the rags themselves in the sun and wind, in a moment of arrest. In this moment of arrest we become aware that there exists a nation between Naples and the Sea of China, between Modena and India, between Fez and San Francisco. A nation of men, women, and children who live, suspended on a line that this ephemeral condition of existence is but the definition of a way of living and therefore not a drama. Thus it is proof itself that life exists.

I asked myself if the images of washing machines that burst into this sequence, those automatic ones lined up in a row and that are coin-operated in low-cost laundromats in the industrial peripheries of the world, freeze or cancel the splendor of colors or of the sun.

The answer is no, if the meaning of the rags themselves, of the cloths to be washed and dried is a way of defining and documenting life. The penumbrous interior of the laundromats is a continuation, while the protagonists pass in a row across the long, darkened zone of the city. I have never seen a boundary so extreme in the other images as to make me think that the cycle ends here. I have seen too many different representations of what we call life, like a robust plant that takes root and reproduces almost everywhere. This is but a passage in the canyon, and I already know that, first and last, there is always a new ocean breeze, sky and light, and their fury and their joy.

One more thing. It is useless to pretend that this is foreign to poetry: these machines, with their awkward appearance of aliens that seem to enter thus into the rapport between humans and nature have a role that intersects that trajectory. It intersects labor. It liberates women's hands that have made those rags, have dyed those gauzes, offered those cloths to the wind, have hung hammocks in the sun. Remaining on the outside, at the "exterior," the author offers us images of laundromats as if they had been taken from a distance (although these images are among the few "interiors" in this voyage). He presents them in shadow, and it is right that they be so: from now on light belongs to free time.

Thus Suspended on a Line is also a voyage across varying testimonials of human presence and life that depends increasingly less on physical labor as a mark to leave on the planet, as a trace of human passage. Unexpectedly color appears no longer, not any more as the object of a casual beauty, but as the fruit of deliberate, creative acts, the very imprint on existence. The machine, in the dark, has accomplished its work of liberation.

Dear Niso,

I can remember when with father and Enzo you studied the first washing machines, the hesitation in baptizing them with the magical name of "Candy," and then, soon after, the story of our company.

You were the most enthusiastic and convinced and also the most involved.

How would we have come to know washing machines today if you had not taken that path that the rest of the world has followed to some extent? How many of your "finds" are recognized today as the basis for a good product!

How many successes, how much joy, but also how much anxiety! The idea of realizing this book was born to give testimonial to this "small" problem of women and how our desire to help them has spread throughout the world. We have certainly made a major contribution.

We will always think of you with affection and recognition for everything you have given, not only as realization, but as education and example.

From one who loves you and doesn't forget,
Peppino

Eng. Niso Fumagalli, President of Candy,
deceased March 9, 1990

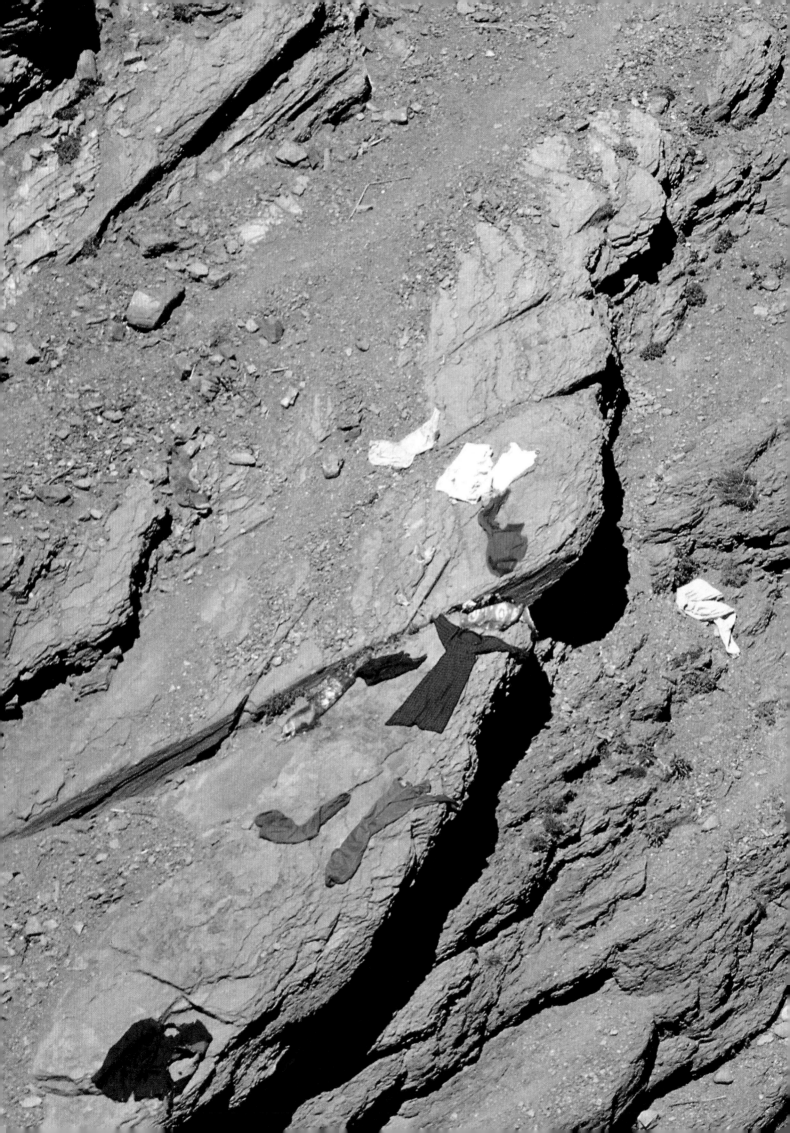

44

Here nobody is rich and
nobody is desperate.
He presents his rags as
a guarantee for next day's
sun, as a continuation
of life, more than as a
declaration of necessity.

At times the concrete

is emphasized, sometimes

the water, sometimes the sky,

or the rag with its more or

less characteristic lightness

and gayety, and its color

that transforms all other

colors.

The human protagonist,
of whom the rags are a
testimonial, can be the
child that is bathing, the
elderly person who sits
waiting, the woman who is
working, the man who
watches.

At first glance I thought the colors were very beautiful, the cleverly cropped, sharp images always suggestive of something about to be revealed while hiding something else.

BIG AL'S
NUDE GIRLS
20's
TOTALLY NUDE
GIRLS ON STA
ACT
BIG AL'S
TOW AWAY
NO STOPPING
SATIONAL

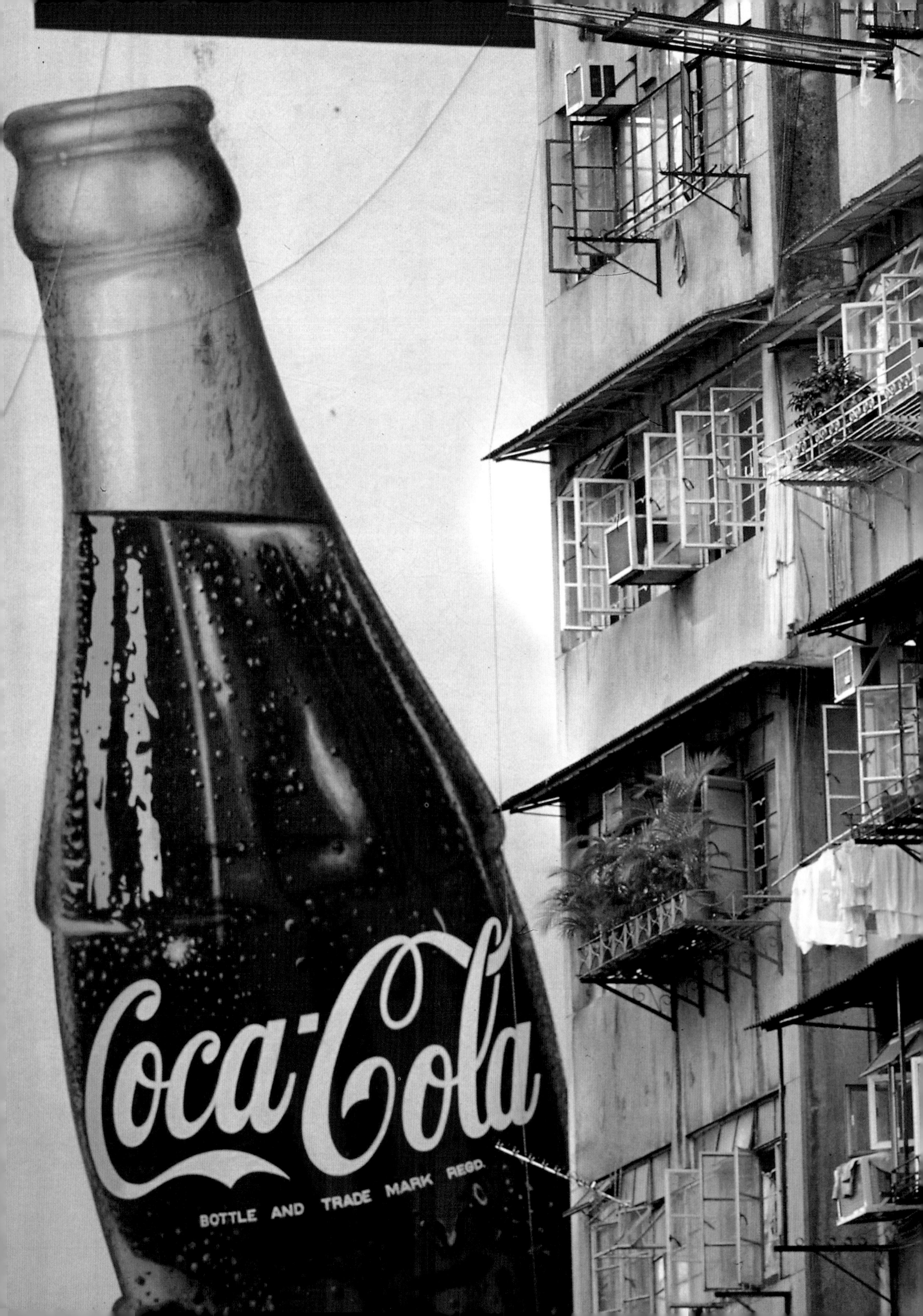
Coca-Cola
BOTTLE AND TRADE MARK REGD.

Here intuition is so
simple as to appear
banal: the rags
themselves, left by
someone for whatever
reason, are always a
proof of life. This is
a reason in itself.

This makes way for
the presence of water,
earth and sky. The wind
and natural phenomena burst
forth blowing up and changing
the shape of things, and
someone who lives in
contact with nature is in
a good position to understand
them as natural facts.

131

The sign of life is pursued

in a way that is simple,

primitive and infallible: the

washed rag, the clean, threadbare

or faded rag. Rags, cloth,

sheets, gauze, hammock, as

signs of life and survival.

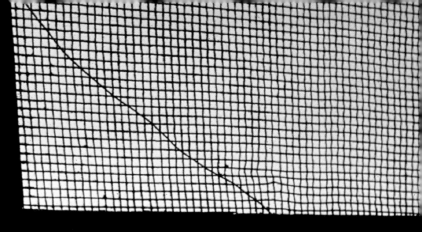

The rags in the wind

are a sign of existence

and continuity of life,

they are the reassuring proof

that someone is close by,

with their work, their

shelter, their children,

their resting place . . . .

We need to come closer,

go further in. And farther

away. We need to discover

where each part of the

encoded message in each

photograph, each color, and

each rag will take us.

About the Photographer

Walter Battistessa was born in Saronno, Italy in 1948 and now resides in Milan. He began working as a photographer in 1967 at the age of nineteen. In 1971 he published an extensive report in the Italian magazine *Abitare*, on the condition of the handicapped in Europe. In 1973 he showed images of the world of surgery and social causes in Italy at the Galleria "Il Diaframma" in Milan. He began an extended collaboration with the Italian and international press documenting the salient customs of the 1970s and 1980s.

His reports concern student movements, the birth and growth of the music festival phenomenon, the status of women, labor, the rise of consumerism, the condition of youth, the earthquake in Friuli, etc. At the invitation of Lanfranco Colombo he participated in various cultural divisions of the SICOF (Salone Internaz. Cinefotottica Milano). He shot stadium events for the Italian group of The Concerned Photographer and has illustrated various encyclopedias, including the Rizzoli Larousse. Among his portfolios, published by the top magazines in the field, are the pop festival in Europe, the condition of children in Sweden, the end of the dictatorship in Greece, and Spain after Franco. In the 1980s he became actively involved in the promotion and appraisal of photojournalism in Italy with the Gruppo Telecinefotoreporters dell' Associazione Lombarda.

Group Shows
3 Weltausstellung der photographie–Stern, an exhibition on the condition of man in our century, traveling to 367 museums in 51 countries.
Venezia 79–La Fotografia–Electa Editrice: L'informazione negata (Suppressed information), curated by Uliano Lucas and Maurizio Bizziccari.
L'occhio di Milan (The eye of Milan), 48 photographs from 1945 to 1977, Milano Rotonda della Besana.
Reporter a Milano, from 1968 to 1982, Palazzo Dugnani in Milan.
Autoscatto (Auto release) 1956/1986, thirty years of photographs and cars, Forum Piazza Carignano, Turin.
Chi troppo e chi niente (Someone and no one), a show on fame, curated by the Centro Diaframma Canon.
Tra sogno e bisogno (Between dream and necessity), 306 photographs and thirteen essays on the evolution of Italian customs, from 1940 to 1986, curated by Cesare Colombo.
Italy: One hundred years of photography, an exhibition of 100 years of Italian photography traveling to major American cities, curated by the Smithsonian Institution.
La fabbrica delle imagini (Factory of images), Italian industry in art photography, Ed. Alinari. His photographs are placed in the central study and communications archive at the University of Parma. From 1979 to 1981 he was photographer at *Corriere della Sera*. He was picture consultant for important industrial companies, realizing reports and audiovisual monographs. In the 1980s he documented the rise of the computer. In 1987, in Milan at the United States Information Center, he presented the show of black-and-white photography: *Marilyn Merlot: Appunti su New York* (Marilyn Merlot: Notes on New York), currently traveling in Italy and other countries. He is currently involved with fashion, advertising, and portraiture, specifically for the magazine *Capital* published by Rizzoli in Milan.

1. Village of Sanganer, Rajasthan, India

2. 3. Dyer's souk, Marrakech, Morocco

4. 5. The laundry of a Berber nomad tribe near the High Atlas, Morocco

6. 7. Dyer's souk, Marrakech, Morocco

8. 9. In the countryside of New South Wales, Australia

10. 11. Village of Fie at Sciliar, Trentino Alto Adige, Italy

12. 13. Causeway Bay, Hong Kong

14. 15. Elizabeth Arden store, Rodeo Drive, Los Angeles

16. 17. Jaipur, Rajasthan, India

18. 19. The Ganges at Varanasi, India

20. 21. Women of the High Atlas wash a carpet in an uidian near the village of Quarzazate, Morocco

23. Artisan dyeworks at Sanganer, Rajasthan, India

24. 25. A "sadu" strolls his ghat at the Ganges, Varanasi, India

26. 27. Island of Gheung Chau, Hong Kong

28. 29. District of Oaxaca, Mexico

30. 31. The ghat of the Ganges, Varanasi, India

32. 33. On the terraces of the city, Marrakech, Morocco

34. 35. Cemetery, Fez, Morocco

36. 37. Courtyard of a house, Fez, Morocco

38. 39. On the ghat of the Ganges, Varanasi, India

40. 41. Nashville, Tennessee

42. From left to right and from top to bottom: New Orleans, Los Angeles, New Orleans, Nashville, San Francisco/Sausalito, San Francisco/Berkeley, Atlanta, Atlanta

43. New Orleans, Louisiana

44. 45. Pennsylvania

46. 47. Lancaster, Pennsylvania

48. 49. Lancaster, Pennsylvania

50. Los Angeles, California

51. Jaselmer, Rajasthan, India

52. 53. Queensland, Australia

54. Brisbane, Australia (above)
Alto Adige, Italy (below)

55. Village of Marken, Holland

56. 57. Countryside in Modena, Italy

58. An Indian woman in the district of Chiapas, Mexico

60. 61. A peasant woman in the valley of the Dades, Morocco

62. 63. Inside the houses of Jaselmer, Rajasthan, India

64. 65. Interior of the Casbah, Village of Quarzazate, Morocco

66. 67. Homemade clothes, New Delhi, Rajasthan, India

68. 69. Jaselmer, Rajasthan, India

71. The son of a horse breeder, Queensland, Australia

72. 73. Indians of the village of Mitla, Chiapas, Mexico

74. 75. Fez, Morocco

76. Dawn at Varanasi, India

77. Island of Cheung Chau, Hong Kong (above)
On a junk on Causeway Bay, Hong Kong (below)

78. 79. In a Casbah at Tineghir, Morocco

81. Jodhpur, Rajasthan, India

82. 83. Varanasi, India

84. 85. Varanasi, India

86. 87. The countryside south of Rajasthan, India

88. 89. Varanasi, India

90. 91. Varanasi, India

92. 93. Varanasi, India

94. 95. Varanasi, India

96. Small batik factory in Jodhpur, Rajasthan, India

98. 99. Varanasi, India

100. 101. Varanasi, India

102. 103. Varanasi, India

104. 105. San Francisco, California

106. 107. Heidelberg, Germany

108. 109. Wanchai Quarter, Hong Kong

110. 111. Hong Kong

112. 113. Kowloon, Hong Kong

114. 115. Stanley Village, Hong Kong

116. 117. Countryside, Morocco

118. 119. Fez, Morocco

121. Village of Volendam, Holland, The Netherlands

122. Casbah in the gorge of Ziz, Morocco

123. Island of Burano, Italy

124. 125. Island of Burano, Italy

126. 127. Andalusia, Spain

128. Reggio Emilia, Italy

129. Spanish Quarter, Naples, Italy

131. San Francisco, California

132. Via Caracciolo, Naples, Italy (above)
Sanita Quarter, Naples, Italy (below)

133. Los Angeles, California (above)
Island of Burano, Italy (below)

135. Shelter for pilgrims along the ghat, Varanasi, India

136. 137. Amalfi, Italy

138. 139. Surfers Paradise, Australia

140. 141. Camp along the Corallina Boundary near Brisbane, Australia

142. 143. The countryside of New South Wales, Australia

144. 145. A jakaroo north of Queensland, Australia

146. 147. Naples, Italy

148. 149. Yucatan, Mexico

150. 151. Positano, Italy

152. Venice, Italy (above)
Naples, Italy (below)

154. 155. Pontoon bridge on the Rhine at Cologne, Germany

156. 157. A junk on the bay of Aberdeen, Hong Kong

158. 159. A fisherman at Causeway Bay, Hong Kong

160. 161. The cotton of a small factory is dried at a street
           intersection, New Delhi, India

162. 163. Rajasthan, India

164. 165. A laundry, Village of Bikaner, India

     166. Jaipur, Rajasthan, India

     167. Udaipur, Rajasthan, India

168. 169. Buddhist priests, India

170. 171. Perigord, France

172. 173. Jaselmer, Rajasthan, India

174. 175. Village in the desert of Thar, India

     176. Countryside in Queensland, Australia

     177. Village of Nimbimbi, Australia

     179. District of Veracruz, Mexico

180. 181. New South Wales, Australia

182. 183. Campeche, Mexico

184. 185. Berbers of the High Atlas, Morocco

186. 187. Peasant women of Puebla, Mexico

188. 189. Public fountain at Fez, Morocco

     190. Island of Burano, Italy

     191. New York City

     192. San Francisco, California